Barack Obama
George W. Bush
&
The American Dream

"George Obama"

B. Charles Henry

Contents

Preface

The American dream is deeply rooted in the American system of government. It therefore behooves governments, and in particular, heads of governments, to provide the modus, stimulus, and opportunities necessary to make that dream possible and to keep it alive. This dream is rooted in the vision, passion, and foresight of the founding fathers of this great land called America through the greatest document that has ever been written regarding the state of affairs for the ordinary man.

Indeed, these great men, persons such as Bartlett and others of New Hampshire, Hancock and others of Massachusetts, Hopkins and Ellery of Rhode Island, Sherman and others of Connecticut, and Floyd and others of New York, one of the greatest cities of all times that realistically represents the ideals of this truly marvelous document called the Declaration of Independence of the United States of America.

Of equal import are the contributions of so many others from New Jersey, Pennsylvania, Delaware, Maryland, Virginia, North Carolina, South Carolina, and Georgia. These brave and fearless men crafted the most worthy document in any period throughout history that continues to strengthen and encourage forgotten, forsaken, and trampled individuals all across the world in these supposedly modern and contemporary times. The lived experiences of so many individuals fall short of unalienable rights, equality, and justice for all.

But are the ideals of the American Dream changing? How does the performance of the President impacts such Dream? A brief analysis of both Presidents George W. Bush and Barrack Hussein Obama may provide some guidance to these two questions. It may also be important to note how the political parties themselves may contribute to the effective functioning of the office of the President and, by extension, how domestic and foreign policy decisions are arrived at.

The American Dream may be interpreted from multiple perspectives and therefore no single definition would provide adequate justice to the term. Notwithstanding, the term in this context is used to mean freedom, justice, brotherhood, peace, and equality for individuals whether they be resident aliens, green card holders, citizens, or whatever other terms one may use to justify the existence of persons living in the United States. As such, the term implies that there exist freedom of religion, of assembly, to bear arms, to enjoy a reasonable lifestyle, to express personal political opinions, and the plethora of other individual rights and freedom supposedly ought to be available to man.

However, is there existing confusion surrounding this Dream? Because certainly, freedom cannot mean free will to act and to do whatever one wants whenever one wants. No civil society could exist in such circumstances. As Mead, the philosopher proffered, the unitary "I" that Descartes (philosopher) posited is an incomplete picture of self because the self is neither autonomous nor complete. Mead argued that there is "the 'I' (the subject self) and the 'me' (the object of consideration for others.)"

Mead opined that the "I" and the "me" seek two separate set of facts but the "me" supersedes because the "I" satisfy the self whereas the "me" belong to the group. Therefore, the "me" construct meaning within the context of such group.

To see this Dream in any other way would annihilate civilization. Anarchy and civilized living would be inconsequential if there is no group. Mead noted that the psychology of self lends focus to "the internal coherence and development of the psyche" of one's soul and being.

Therefore, the proper functioning of the state and any influence that a President may have require cooperation and collaboration among contending and competing interests for the sake of the whole. Whether Bush or Obama, the realities still remain unchanged. Here again, this is not to take away from any folly that either men may have done. Although no man is perfect, there is no excuse for expensive stupidity, and too often, the world is confronted with what seem to be obvious distortions to specific unalienable rights, the kinds so eloquently espoused in the great document alluded to earlier.

Since the 1933 modification of the US constitution, the inaugural date for swearing in the incoming President has changed from March 4 to January 20. This gives the incoming President very little time to transition from a candidate to taking the oath for the most powerful office in the world. During that brief period from November 4, the date of the results, to January 4, the date to assume office, the President must correctly accomplish a series of activities if his transition into the Presidency is to be successful. Therefore, part of the measuring stick for assessing both Bush and Obama must be this transition period. An unprepared leader may not be able to accomplish substantial achievement for keeping the American Dream alive. After all, the President is the leader of the free world. He should be able to demonstrate in no uncertain terms, his abilities to lead, because leadership is about achieving stated and intended objectives.

Effective leaders must come with the appropriate abilities or traits, must be able to situate themselves felicitously, and be willing to radically transform their organizations or their countries. Leaders of contemporary times must be visionaries.

Kotter, a social scientist, noted that leadership is "the process of moving a group (or groups) in some direction through mostly noncoercive means." Leadership, especially in times of trying circumstances, should endeavor to reach within their inner being and bring about the kinds of abilities that provide exceptional guidance, motivation, influence, and success. Yukl, a social scientist, posited that the transformational leader use leadership "as transforming the values and priorities of followers and motivating them to perform beyond their expectations." Exceptional leadership empowers their followers in a way that help them to achieve goals beyond their own abilities.

The American Dream is therefore a combination of exceptional leadership and followership that foster and engender the notions espoused in the Declaration of Independence.

The lived experiences of followers are essential to establishing justification for such ideals. Presidents and electors alike must understand this relationship, cooperate, and collaborate on the affairs of the country to achieve the noble expectations of the founding fathers of the great USA.

Author's Biography

The author originates from the West Indies. He holds a Bachelor of Science degree with majors in Accounting and Management Studies and a Master of Science degree in Computer Based Management Information Systems. The author is currently pursuing doctoral studies in Organizational Leadership with specialization in Information Systems and Technology.

The author is an Information Technology Manager and an Adjunct Lecturer in various information systems courses within a for profit university. The author achieved the Who's Who of Professionals recognition in 2001. In 2002, he was nominated a Mover and Shaker in the premier local daily West Indian newspaper. He is a full member of IEEE Computer Society and a member of the local computer society.

The Presidents

1

George W. Bush

George W. Bush, the 43rd President, himself the son of a former President, George H. W. Bush, must have been in a very good position to take the nomination for the Republican Party in 2000. After all, he has the requisite ties to a family that know how to get to the White House. He is the eldest son of the 41st President of the United States. Born July 6, 1946, Bush became the second son to join his father as President. The only other person to have such a feat is John Quincy Adams who became the sixth President of the United States in 1825. His father, John Adams was the second President of the United States.

Bush, the Governor of Texas at the time, the largest of the contiguous states, should have been in a good position to take the country forward.

The Governor is the executive of a state, so he should have the requisite executive experience, all be it on a smaller scale to what is expected at the national level. Bush is also a graduate of the prestigious Yale University. He is married to a wonderful wife, Laura Welch and has two beautiful daughters, Barbara and Jenna.

Bush was born in Connecticut but was raised in Texas along with his other siblings Jeb, Neil, Marvin, and Dorothy. Jeb, of course, was a successful Governor of Florida. Bush's family has a long history in politics. His grandfather Prescott was a US Senator whereas his father served the United States both as Vice President and as President respectively. He attended public schools in Midland, Texas prior to relocating to Houston where he attended Kinkaid Preparatory. He attended the all male boarding high school Phillips Academy in Massachusetts. Bush always insisted that he is an average performer in school. Bush went on to the prestigious Harvard University where he pursued his MBA making him the only US President with an MBA.

George bush is an avid businessman and spent some of his early years investing in the oil industry. He operated many small oil exploration companies. He also invested in sport, becoming part owner of the Texas Rangers and served the organization as its managing general partner for five years.

During his period as Governor of Texas, George Bush enacted new laws to allow Texans to carry concealed weapons and used the existing surplus budget to enact the largest tax cut in Texan history, an amount of two billion dollars. He provided government funding to institutions for alcohol and drug abuse users, and for persons who suffer domestic violence. He encouraged and supported faith-based organizations, and used his Christian faith to influence others to serve. He is the first Governor of Texas to be elected to two consecutive four years term.

His road to the Presidency seemed imminent. The media always focused on him as a possible candidate for the White House and so his announcement in 1999 was hardly surprising. It helped that no incumbent Republican was in the White House.

Bush won 29 of the 50 states in his first national election including the controversial state of Florida where the US Supreme Court that handed the election victory over to Bush took the final decision. The recount in Florida showed Bush beating Gore by 537 votes whereas Gore had won the popular national votes by 543,895. Because of the Supreme Court decision, Bush got the majority of Electoral College votes, 271 to be exact, to become the 43rd United States President.

Barack Hussein Obama II

Barack Hussein Obama II originates from the picturesque and warm state of Hawaii in the Pacific Ocean. Born to a black African father and a white American mother, the eloquent Obama seemed to have set sight on the national job for some time. He is a graduate of the prestigious ivy leagues Columbia University and Harvard University and is the 44th President of the United States. Within the context of the existing racial culture of the United States, his victory to the White House demonstrates an exceptional ability on his part. His fellow compatriots must have gleaned a sense of hope and aspiration they thought previously impossible.

Prior to ascending to the Presidency, Obama served as a US Senator from Illinois. He is married to a wonderful wife Michelle Robinson and has two beautiful daughters Malia and Sasha. His Hawaiian birth has, from time to time, proved challenging to accept for his opponents as they regularly question the modern birth certificate provided by the State of Hawaii.

Intensive investigations surrounding this matter however corroborated the facts as recorded on his birth paper.

Obama spent four years of his early childhood between the ages of six and ten attending school in Indonesia. At 10 years old, Obama returned to Hawaii to live with his maternal grandparents and attended a preparatory high school. After completing high school, Obama moved to California where he attended Occidental College in Los Angeles. During his teenage years, his mother was spending time between Hawaii and Indonesia.

After leaving college, Obama worked as a community organizer in Chicago where he helped to establish a job-training program for individuals of little means. He later went on to Harvard where he pursued his JD. This qualification equipped him to become a visiting professor at University of Chicago. Establishing himself in Chicago, Obama was able to hone in and capitalize on his connections that likely helped him to become a Senator for the state. This was the beginning of his journey to the White House.

During his time as a Senator, Obama sought support from the opposing party for laws to reform ethics and health. He sponsored laws reducing the tax burden on low-income individuals and participated in efforts to reform welfare. Obama objected to the War in Iraq. He is the only member of the Congressional Black Caucus to become a Senator. On February 10, 2007, Obama announced his candidacy for the job of the 44th President of the United States. The location of his announcement was carefully selected to reflect the ideals of Abraham Lincoln. Lincoln had previously warned in a 1858 speech in Illinois "a house divided against itself cannot stand." Obama's campaign projected the theme of *hope* and *change*.

Domestic Policies

The politics of D.C. have a profound impact on the American Dream. Electors therefore have a duty to influence both the decisions and actions of their representatives. The contemporaneous tea party movement in vogue has a right to actions although some activities may be considered inappropriate but that too is a right not only guaranteed by the US constitution but it is also eloquently etched in the document of the Declaration of Independence. Others who may wish to see different decisions should form similar groupings and demand their five minutes in the limelight. For the survival of the American Dream, its founding documents must remain meaningful to those who seek such Dream.

There are certain fundamental facts required to support and foster continued survival of any economy. Leaders must provide the necessary infrastructure so that the enterprising can have a foundation upon which to build.

The 21st century demands a technological solution to job creation steeped in efficiencies and effectiveness. Education is a necessity. Without appropriate education, it is not likely that the average worker will be equipped to assume the challenges of contemporary America. Medical costs must be adequately managed so that all persons have a fair chance at receiving appropriate and adequate healthcare. Work must be meaningful and worth the effort. Individuals will not be motivated to conduct themselves with tasks that have miniscule returns. Therefore, better paying jobs must be found. There must be fairness in how firms and individuals alike are treated. Their taxes must be seen as equitable. Persons must have secure identity. Technology must be applied to existing systems to provide such guarantee to individuals. The excessive investment in wars overseas comes at the expense of the domestic economy. These wars must be minimized to the absolute necessity so that those funds can become more readily available to the domestic economy for both capital and recurrent expenditures. Something effective has to be done to the speculators on Wall Street.

They are unjustly driving up investment costs. Whatever it takes to strengthen the democratic process must be done. Weak democracies provide too many opportunities to foster corruption. Corruption is an expensive venture for any economy.

How presidents set their agenda is important to what they will achieve and, by extension, how serious the congress will treat such agenda. It is not too early to point out however, that there exist limitations on what a President can achieve. Quite a bit of actions exists outside the realm of the executive branch of government.

Nevertheless, Presidents should be aware that their success is endogenous to the domestic issues they pursue because they always consider the actions of congress prior to pursuing any specific issues. Their misreading therefore cannot be an excuse to lackluster performance.

George W Bush

President Bush domestic agenda zeroed in on tax cuts, education reform, and the expansion of energy production. However, these foci may have been somewhat shifted because of the attack of September 11, 2001. Notwithstanding, he achieved much success. Within the first week of his presidency, Bush requested tax cuts for $1.6 trillion dollars over a period of 10 years. Greenspan, the Federal Board Chairman at the time, advised that although the economy was slowing, such cuts were not detrimental. Greenspan noted that the cuts might actually have a positive effect on the economy. The final bill the president signed required him to compromise on fundamental disagreement, but this seems to be the beast of Washington. Without such compromise, nothing gets accomplished. In signing the tax bill, Bush noted that one could achieve objectives that move from political impossibility to reality. This was a major achievement for Bush to boost economic activities.

The President's second achievement was the passing of the No Child Left Behind Act. Although some may remain skeptical such as the National Education Association, the legislation enjoyed strong bipartisan support. The same success cannot be said of the Katrina disaster however. The Katrina debacle in Louisiana proved disastrous for Bush with both FEMA and the President irking many previously strong Bush supporters. The extended war in Iraq did not help the President either.

In addressing the constant immigration problems of the United States, Bush opined that illegal immigrants should be given temporary worker status. He argued that to do otherwise, such as extending amnesty to undocumented workers is to encourage individuals to constantly break the laws of the United States. This did not prevent the President to recognize the importance of immigration in keeping the American Dream alive. He acknowledged the importance of remaining a welcoming society.

Barack Hussein Obama II

The domestic agenda of Obama seemed to be consumed with the ongoing recession. His sizable stimulus package, notwithstanding arguments relating to size and efficacy, is one of his larger achievements. Only time will prove the long-term effect of such a stimulus package. The President also enacted programs to stop or delay foreclosures and to provide affordable homes. Strong arguments exist both for and against these initiatives, but that is the order of politics. The virtue of the politician only comes with history.

The financial meltdown in recent past seems not to have escaped observers. There are those who argue that another recession is on the horizon. How the President respond will be crucial to the direction the economy takes. The President noted that his efforts to bail out financial institutions have saved the country from a second great depression.

Two other substantial achievements for Obama include the reduction of student loan subsidies by a whopping $400 billion and the successful efforts of his health care reforms. In addition, Obama has signed into law the Ledbetter Fair Pay Act and routed additional funds toward workplace safety programs.

Obama gave the green light to open new drilling sites along the Atlantic coastline, Alaska's north coast, and the eastern Gulf of Mexico. This is a significant decision that will lessen the demand for foreign produced oil and natural gas over time. Because of the strong support Obama received from Hispanic voters to the ascendancy of his Presidency, he remains lackluster in his priorities for illegal immigrants and undocumented workers. The President has endured strong criticisms for his approach to matters of immigration.

Similarities & Differences

Both Presidents have demonstrated support for harnessing more oil and natural gas domestically. However, in addition to wanting more local production, Obama wants a greater contribution to energy from renewable sources. Both men believe that illegal workers in the country should be accommodated, notwithstanding the different approach taken by each. One wants amnesty, the other does not. The Obama administration differ substantially in how it treats political issues by proposing multiple bold initiatives concurrently whereas the Bush administration would be more cautious, advancing one or two major issues simultaneously.

Nevertheless, Bush has never failed to support the President, first by ensuring a smooth transition for the incoming President to the White House. Second, by keeping his promise of secrecy to the President, Obama can have confidence in seeking his advice if needed. In the final analysis, both men are the 43rd and 44th Presidents of the extraordinary United States of America.

3 Foreign Policies

Not only does what happen in Washington affects the response to the local economy but also the decisions taken about what obtains aboard. To a large extent, decisions affecting external entities have huge financial consequences. If one examine the two extended wars for example, Afghanistan and Iraq, it would not be unreasonable to decipher their impact on other decisions affecting America such as the cost for education, health, housing, transportation, infrastructure, and even other government bureaucracies.

America is one of the largest contributors, if not the largest, in every global institutions of which it is a part. The US contribution to NATO is 22% to its civil budget, 22% to its military budget, and 22% to its security investment program (SNIP). The closest and only other double-digit contributor is the United Kingdom contributing 13%, 12%, and 12% respectively.

America's contribution to the United Nations is 22% and the only other double-digit contributor is Japan, contributing 19% to the UN budget. The United States has the largest quota at the IMF, contributing 18% to the fund. This is not to imply that these contributions and participation at the level occurring is not reasonable or necessary, but it does say that some of the resources that would have otherwise been available to domestic issues are no longer, because however rich one may find oneself, wealth is not a limitless phenomenon. The more resources allocated to foreign use the less that remain to achieve domestic government responsibilities.

Oil is a huge sour point in America. Oil is one of the cornerstones of the economy, yet so many of it comes from abroad. Oil may also remain one of the greatest influences on foreign policy decisions. So many of the wars fought seem to be associated with oil. Maybe the push to more domestic production may assist in lessening these conflicts in future endeavors.

In the current scenario, the Middle Eastern countries with roughly 50% of the total oil reserve provide substantial quantities of the commodity to the global economy and much of that comes to the United States. This area of the world has strong US government military presence. A reasonable question to ask therefore would seem to be whether there exist any link between the demand for oil and the strong military presence in that region.

An important note to the oil debacle is that OPEC has a strong influence on oil prices and output and has demonstrated this ability from time to time. What therefore, can be done to influence the decision-makers of this Austria based organization peacefully and soberly? Some of the OPEC members are not necessarily eager to become friends of the Americans. The current member countries include such states as Qatar, Libya, the United Arab Emirates, Algeria, Nigeria, Angola, Iran, Kuwait, Saudi Arabia, and Venezuela. The public discourse between the United States, Iran, and Venezuela and, by extension, their feelings toward each other is no secret. One needs only to assess the presentations of Achmadenijad and Chavez to the United Nations.

This is not to criticize the goodly gentlemen because it remains their fundamental right to speak their minds, but such relationships are tenuous at best. If the world is truly to be a global village transcending cultures, races, class, and other informal distinctions between human beings, then world leaders must collaborate. There is no prerequisite to like each other. However, the common good of mankind demand that the contemporary world should cooperate.

The United States has established itself as the world's police force and therefore the worldview of the US should be important to its leaders. Too often US leadership seems to misinterpret the views of others as negative to the values of America. In most cases, that understanding is false. Usually, the views of America generally stop with policy makers, that is, decisions affecting persons outside the United States are seen as bad, not that the American value system is bad. American leaders therefore have an obligation to understand world cultures in order to make effective decisions that serve their population at an optimum level, guaranteeing equally, rights and security.

According to the 2006 Public Agenda poll, 64% of Americans believe that the worldview of America is negative whereas 24% see America in a positive light. That same poll recorded 73% of Americans worrying about US friendship to the rest of the world. According to this poll, the policies of George Bush contributed to this negative worldview. The research contributed 78% of this reduced goodwill to foreign policies. However, Americans understand the dislike. They believe that the dislike has hardly anything to do with American values. Instead, they interpret the negative outlook on American policies. In other words, Americans view the policies of Washington as threatening their very existence. These policies should be achieving the reverse, making America prosperous and safer.

A similar survey conducted in the Middle East in 2006 confirmed the American interpretation of the negative outlook. Sixty-two percent of respondents in the Middle East agreed with the Americans. Americans are not very comfortable with this current trend because every 9 out of 10 persons want America to be viewed positively by outsiders as gleaned from the 2006 Public Agenda survey.

Correctly stated again, Americans understand their values to be more important in protecting their security given the existing global challenges. In the same survey, 87% believed that if judged on values, America is likely viewed positively by outsiders. One therefore has to ask whether Washington understand this relationship between values and principles, and the consequent actions that D.C. should take.

There are times however, when it may seem counterproductive to argue with the position taken by most American because, on the face of it, conflicting views seem to sway depending on the prevailing circumstances. One would expect such irrationality after the 9/11 attack. It would seem justified during that particular epoch. The Public Agenda survey in 2006 gleaned that in excess of 60% of Americans believed that the country is doing enough for less fortunate states. Interestingly, in the same survey, 64% of Americans believed that it is always wrong to cooperate with dictators when fighting terrorism although they concluded that it might be necessary at times.

The American worldview is realistic to the prevailing circumstances. Maybe the world has not noted and may not be giving them the credit they deserve.

Globalization and Trade

Majority of individuals globally are accepting that globalization is positively related to national economies although many individuals remain ambivalent about the cost of globalization to the environment and to job creation. America remains the predominant consumer of global production and countries bustling with increased output don't seem to mind their new found fame for these benefits. Support in export-oriented countries saw strong correlation for global trade such as 87% in China, 86% in South Korea, 82% in Israel, and 60% in the United States according to the 2007 World Public Opinion research.

George W Bush

The reign of George Bush has seen tension between China and North Korea, a withdrawal for the Kyoto Protocol, and a new law passed, the American Servicemembers' Protection Act to immune military personnel, elected, and appointed officials from ICC prosecution. In addition, he implemented or restored trade restrictions in contravention of the WTO although he signed many agreements directly with individual countries such as Australia, Chile, Oman, Singapore, the Ukraine, and many other countries. There was increased defense spending, a cut of budgetary allocation to international organizations such as the UN, and a reduction in foreign aid. Tanzania however, got massive aid from the former President.

The September 11 act of terrorism has lead to human rights violation, the establishment of the Guantanamo Bay prison in Cuba, and two wars in Iraq and Afghanistan. During the President's reign, Israel bombed Syria. There were unease with Iran, a major conflict between Sudan, and a planned missile defense system for Eastern Europe.

Barack Hussein Obama II

Obama has invested much time in reaching out to the Muslim and Arab world by initiating contact with leaders of Palestine, Israel, Jordon, and Egypt on his first day at the White House. Obama pursued the difficulties associated with the Darfur genocide, Zimbabwe autocracy, and resource conservation across the continent of Africa. He pursued actions in Kenya to address the increased incidence of piracy.

Although Obama's rhetoric toward China would seem to encourage cooperation between the two nations, which is essential for the survival of both countries, at the same time there seems to be a deliberate message to have India strengthens its Asian position to challenge the dominance of China. North Korea appears to be much bolder since the Obama administration than they were previously when expressing public sentiments.

The new surge in civil unrest to remove dictatorial leaders in the Middle East that resulted in the fall of Gaddafi in Libya and the overthrow of Mubarak in Egypt may be encouraging for Obama. Equally of note is the intention for Karzai to step down in 2014.

The President has increased cooperation with Brazil and Canada and has loosened certain restrictions that the US government has previously imposed on Cuba. The President has also vowed to work closer with Venezuela but Chavez seems uncertain as to Obama's gravitas. Notwithstanding the foregoing, Obama's popularity overseas continues to be strong which translates into a positive image of the United States.

According to a Pew Global Attitudes Project, Obama has strong favorability in France 73%, Germany 63%, Russia 57%, China 58%, Japan 66%, South Korea 79%, Poland 74%, Brazil 62%, India 66%, and Indonesia 59%. However, such favorability is very low in Muslim nations such as Pakistan, Turkey, and Egypt where US favorability is 17% in all three states. Mexico, a bordering country with the United States has a favorability rating of only 44%.

Clearly, the harsh economic circumstances of contemporary America are not helping the current situation.

Similarities & Differences

Contrary to what obtains during the Bush era, substantial approval obtains for anti-terrorist activities from countries such as the United Kingdom, France, Spain, Germany, Russia, Indonesia, Kenya, Brazil, India, and Nigeria, according to the Pew Global Attitudes Project.

Obama, like Bush, has reiterated a call for a Palestinian state without explaining exactly what that is supposed to be. He, like Bush, emphasized the need for a road map on existing settlements. According to Noam Chomsky, Obama presents himself to the Muslim world in a friendly and engaging way that allow these individuals to project their hopes but for which very little is likely. Overall, Bush seemed more forthright with his rhetoric whereas Obama seem to leave one to guesses.

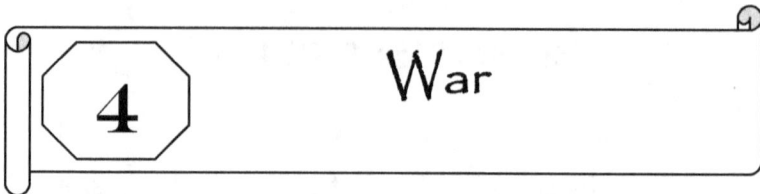

War

War is not an unknown phenomenon for the United States. One could easily argue that had it not been for war, the USA would never have existed. But what a great country it has turned out to be. The principle on which the United States based it first major war is steeped in a noble ideal so eloquently documented in its Declaration of Independence. The document stated that whereas governments exist to secure unalienable rights of individuals such as life, liberty, and the pursuit of happiness, the population has an equal responsibility to alter, abolish, or even institute new governments should government become destructive to the cause and purposes for which they were established to fulfill. These sentiments seem to be the cause for the uprising now taking place in the Middle East. People demand their unalienable rights and will endeavor to achieve them using whatever means they deemed appropriate.

The American Revolutionary war in the latter 18th century between the then 13 British colonies and Great Britain influenced actions taken by other European powers. This war was the result of the British Parliament, which is sovereign to the people, imposing a tax on its colonies that the colonies deemed unconstitutional. The Americans boycott of British tea led to Massachusetts loosing self-government status.

The French, Spanish, and Dutch all lend support to the revolutionaries. However, Britain, having more experience with war than the revolutionaries, entered from Canada, and secured a temporary victory. France was not too pleased about the direction in which the conflict was moving and openly joined the revolutionaries against Great Britain. So too did its allies Spain and the Dutch Republic. The French assistance although successful for America, ruined its own economy. Can any American therefore second-guess the assistance given to France and the larger Europe through the Marshall Plan after World War II?

At the initiation of the American Revolution, the Americans were at a disadvantage when compared to Great Britain. However, the Actions of the Americans attracted many allies whereas the Britons got none. The Americans, unlike other colonies, could survive off their own production and used that fact to their advantage. In addition, the Americans had established effective local and state governments and an efficient communication system. With these efficiencies, the negatives were easily outweighed and in the end, America has done very well for itself and sometimes, for others too.

World War I has seen the entrance of the United States in yet another war. This time however, the reasons were quite different. Until 1917, the USA has stayed neutral but because of the actions of Germany, the Americans were drawn into the war to defend themselves after repeated U-boat attacks on their merchant ships. Notwithstanding, other reasons were also evident such as the huge investments the United States have with Britain and France, political influence from outsiders, and the ideology of President Wilson to provide a safer democratic world.

By the time World War II came along, much have changed. There was a tripartite pact in place between Germany, Italy, and Japan which stated that should any country, except the USSR, declare war on one, they would automatically be participating in that war against the enemy state. Therefore, when Japan attacked Hawaii at Pearl Harbor, a state of war existed between the tripartite pact and the USA. This led both Italy and Germany to declare war against the United States. The USA was now fully a part of the war taking place in Europe.

Other compelling reasons for entering WWII was that in 1940, the United States signed the Lend-Lease act, thereby removing itself from being neutral. The Japanese attack on China in 1931 infuriated the Russians, which would also have upset the Americans because both countries were allies at the time. The German attack on US vessels in the Atlantic, and the fact that Americans were killed in the Pearl Harbor assault by Japan are two additional reasons.

George W Bush

The Presidency of George Bush changed drastically because of the terrorist attack on 9/11, one of the most dreadful acts to have been committed on American soil. This attack led to a massive assault on the Taliban and Al-Qaeda in Afghanistan.   Al-Qaeda owned up to the atrocities of the September 11 attack and therefore justification existed for pursuing their members wherever they were embedded.

But fighting a war in Afghanistan is not a simple feat. The Soviet Union may have still existed had it not been for the time, effort, and money expended on fighting with Afghanistan in addition to favoring totalitarianism over democracy and choosing communism above capitalism. *Perestroika* and *glasnost* may have arrived too late to save the USSR.

Notwithstanding the foregoing, the Afghan war may have been planned prior to the 9/11 attack. According to "What Really Happened," both India and Iran announced in June 2001 that if the economic sanctions did not produce expected results with the Taliban, they would support "limited military actions" by the USA and Russia.

The Afghan war started by Bush was the first major conflict of the 21st century. The length of the war has surpassed that of Vietnam. The war in Vietnam lasted under nine years. However, at the end of his Presidency, the largest and most wanted target for his Afghan mission, Osama bin Laden, was still at large. The mission to either capture or kill him, up to the point of his departure from office, had failed.

In 2002, George Bush increased his rhetoric and enunciated the now popular "axis of evil" term particularly in relation to Iran, Iraq, and North Korea and launched his second war in 2003 against Iraq. Saddam Hussein was deposed and later discovered and hanged.

The Iraqi war saw thousands of civilians being killed during the invasion. However, that did not dampen the spirit of the President. He felt that victory was a certainty.

The Iraqi war was unpopular globally and Bush got his fair share of criticism for waging the war. The war was declared on the pretext that Iraq had weapons of mass destruction. No such weapons were ever found.

Barack Hussein Obama II

It is fair to say that Obama inherited two wars, Iraq and Afghanistan. However, he voted against the Iraqi war while in the Senate and had promised to remove combat troops from Iraq when elected. This was to have been accomplished in 18 months. He missed that deadline.

As regards Afghanistan, Obama had promised to make the country the emphasis of his war efforts and noted that he would shift troupes from Iraq to Afghanistan. He noted his disgust that bin Laden was still at large and of the expansion of the Taliban into Pakistan.

The President has followed up on these stated targets by expanding operations not only in Afghanistan, but also in Pakistan and in the process, capturing and killing bin Laden in Pakistan. Notwithstanding that the Pakistani national sovereignty was breached in the process.

Similarities & Differences

Obama seemed calmer and not one easily flustered. This approach to leadership has won him and his country support from aboard. Bush seems to be less tolerant of these characteristics. However, both leaders seem steadfast in their beliefs.

Obama seems to think that war is to be used as a last resort whereas Bush appears to be less patient. Bush appears to be consistent in his treatment with both rogue nations and allies whereas Obama seem to be more selective on an individual basis. For example, the President rebalanced his position on Mubarak and Ben Ali by withdrawing support and by keeping silent on the occurrences in Yemen and Bahrain.

Libya, on the other hand, seems to have received the full brunt of his frustration with democracy and freedom in the area.

Nevertheless, Obama's approach to diplomacy have won favor with world leaders and in the process, American sentiments abroad have strengthened. From this policy perspective, the improved positive view of America can only be beneficial for future cooperative relation and actions with allies and enemy alike.

5 Democrats v Republicans

A vibrant democracy needs competition, and two party systems across the English world have shown that enough balance can be brought in place to both support and oppose each other on matters of substance. The Democrats and the Republicans are the mainstay parties of the American electoral process and have been keeping democracy alive in the country for two and a half centuries.

The Republican Party

The Republican Party promised and offered ideals of unity, dignity, and human rights. The party encourages courage against foreign adversary, optimism and patriotism to freedom, devotion to human dignity and rights, and the preservation of law that protects liberty.

Republicans believe that the defense of the nation is paramount, and therefore anything deemed necessary to protect the state should be pursued. The party believes that the nation's border should be protected and that amnesty should not be a path to citizenship. George Bush echoed this sentiment very clearly when addressing the immigration problems during his leadership.

The Party supports the right to a free Israel. The party believes that the English language should become the official language of the country.

Every other country must be wondering why this is not already the case because it would seem that America is the only country where the national language is not the de facto official language and it must be the only country where citizens have no obligation to use the national language.

The Republicans believe in a large Army and do not believe in obtaining justice through international jurisdictions. The party believes in safeguarding the constitution, rejects special interest spending, rejects social engineering tax codes, and supports lower corporate tax rates.

The Party supports private ballots for workers, rejects federal spending for abortions, supports the right for persons to choose their healthcare plans, supports the right to bear arms, rejects unions between same sex couples, and supports the right for each person to exercise his or her religious beliefs.

The Democratic Party

The Democrats believe that America run the risk of encouraging terrorism when rhetoric is used out of context. Democrats believe that it is the responsibility of government to provide the infrastructure for job creation and education. The Party believes that jumpstarting the economy through government interventions is good for economic growth.

The Democrats believe that healthcare is a shared responsibility between employees, employers, insurers, and government and that secret ballots for employees should ceased. Democrats believe in strong social services and higher taxes. Democrats believe in a national policy for early childcare and the transfer of wealth from the rich to the poor.

The Democratic Party believes that the world would be a better place without nuclear weapons. Democrats also believe in America having a large Army but the administration have cut the defense budget.

The Democrats believe in equality between all Defense personnel irrespective of race, class, color, creed, sex, or orientation.

The Democrats believe that more cooperative and mutual decisions should be taken with allies instead of unilaterally taking decisions that cross national boundaries and are likely to affect the lives of those beyond the shores of the United States. Democrats believe that human actions contribute to climate change.

Democrats believe that the right to bear arms is subject to regulation and that women have the right to an abortion. The Party detests the strong influence of special interest groups and individuals on the electoral process.

Democrats believe that the federal government has a duty to assist fledgling states and they believe that the people of Washington, D.C. should have the same rights as any other United States citizens, including the right to vote.

The Consensus – Politics is the Problem

Both the Democrats and the Republicans, and by extension, there representatives at the executive level, must recognize their own party idiosyncrasies as they pursue service in the name of the American people because, to the average American, whether the President is Republican or Democrat, if his actions are contrary to the country's good, it would have made no difference.

The rail system, for example, in China and Europe move millions of persons cost-effectively yearly whereas the corresponding American system barely crawls with the antiquated and unprofitable Amtrak. Prescription drugs and medical expenses are the highest in the United States among developed countries.

Trillion of dollars are expended yearly on weapons of mass destruction while the country's infrastructure is largely ignored. Special interest groups have huge influence in Washington whether the party in power is Democratic or the Republican. And even while these ills are taking place, the rhetoric continues from both sides of the isle.

It may be time to put back Americas into the picture because, as it stands, it would appear that Washington is for special interest groups and for the politicians. Whether Barack or Bush, too much is beyond their control.

6 The American Dream

What is the American Dream so many sought and when discovered so well guarded? The beauty about the Dream is that no single definition exists. The Dream can be anything an individual makes it to be. Isn't that the epitome of democracy and freedom? To this day in America, there are many dreaming of equality in life experiences, in race relations, in class distinction, in economic opportunities, in social fortitude, and in a plethora of varied desires any one can imagine.

No one anywhere is in doubt about the dollar culture that obtains in the United States and according to Matthew Warshauer, any society dedicated to capitalism lives the maxim "the one who dies with the most toys wins." Americans demand the opportunities to purchase whatever they want, whether those are huge homes, expensive motor vehicles, or exotic vacations, but at what cost?

The era of hard work seemed to have elapsed and now all sorts of ventures are available for "easy money." As a result, all sorts of schemes have sprung about. There is the dishonesty on Wall Street, the collapse of financial institutions, and the fall of Madoff and his ponzi scheme that he ran so successfully for so many years. This quick fix to life expectation was not always the Dream that those before seek. However, the Dream of economic independence seems to have given way to extravagance. Prudence is now a bad word and competing with the neighbor is the fashionable engagement.

Notwithstanding, the American story of moving from the ubiquitous phrase of "rags to riches" continue to guide the American Dream, all be it sometimes distortedly. This popular sentiment of have to have-not has attracted individuals from all corners of the world where new entrants to America expect to demonstrate perseverance, self-discipline, and self-control in achieving their stated goals.

The ubiquity of the expectation of the American Dream is not always viewed as hope, but sometimes is seen as an entitlement, one that should happen for every man, woman, and child existing in this state without the requisite individual input. The rise of popular game shows, sweepstakes, and lotteries provide false hopes for so many who may have the misguided expectation of rags to riches. How long though can this Dream remain a reality under the pretext that entitlement should replace hard work, and that sacrifice is no longer necessary? As Matthew Warshauer pointed out:

> When a 46 years old Korean immigrant was electrocuted by the "L" train line in Chicago, his family sued and won $3 million in damages. Such an award may not seem outlandish if Mr. Lee had simply stepped onto a faulty rail line or bumped into an exposed wire. Instead, he walked home from a party with a blood alcohol level three times the legal limit, decided to walk past three signs that stated "Danger,"

"Keep Out," "Electric Current," then proceeded to urinate on a live rail line.

He was electrocuted instantly. For contributory negligence, the $3 million reward was cut in half.

Could this have been what the founding fathers intended? Certainly, one should take responsibility for one's own actions. But an entitlement culture is busily replacing the well sought after American Dream. This case is by no means unique. Such suits are common in medicine, road accidents, public and private businesses, and even private residences. It is time to realistically reform tort legislation and other contributing laws in the legal system. What has happened during the time Bush was in office. Obama is there now, what is he doing about it?

Bush noted that it is wrong to offer asylum to individuals breaching the laws of the United States and he is correct in this regard. To offer temporary worker status is already compromising the law but it is the lesser of two evils.

It would seem unfair for persons legitimately waiting in line for legal entry into the United States to be punished by the American system.

It has to be punishment for those engaged in *doing the right thing* to be waiting for up to 10 years whereas those who break the law can simply walk into a government institution, do the necessary paperwork, and voila, everything is all right. Would anyone have noticed any similarities between the preceding paragraph and the story of Mr. Lee? Because if you don't, then maybe you are also one of those who believe that the Dream ought to be an entitlement rather than an opportunity to invest into yourself now for later rewards and gratification.

For the American Dream to stay alive, it cannot be a case of everything I do I win. There must be meaningful rewards and punishment and neither Bush nor Obama have stepped up to address the issue in any meaningful way. Matter of factly, vitriolic and passionate debates about the American Dream seem to have had their star in both Pelosi and Reid instead of any of the last two Presidents.

7 Concluding Thoughts

"We hold these truths to be self-evident, that all men are created equal, that they are endowed by their Creator with certain unalienable Rights, that among these are Life, Liberty, and the Pursuit of Happiness. – That to secure these rights, Governments are instituted among Men, deriving their just powers from the consent of the governed, That whenever any Form of Government becomes destructive of these ends, it is the Right of the People to alter or to abolish it, and to institute new Government, laying the foundation on such principles and organizing its powers in such form, as to them shall seem most likely to effect their Safety and Happiness"

It is hard pressed to find a more complete and profound set of words than to extract the above excerpt from the Declaration of Independence to make good a summary about the American Dream.

In these times of neglect by elected leaders, schisms, and rhetoric that they beamed from their lips without regard for their true purpose to secure the requisite infrastructure that guarantee life, liberty, and happiness for all men and women, it should not be very difficult to understand why the Dream has been so terribly misinterpreted and misaligned for so many who seek its reward.

The substance of the American Dream is fading, ignored by both Bush and Obama and is being replaced by an entitlement mentality that cannot provide for continued strength and growth of America, the great land of the free and the comfortable home for the brave.

In this contemporary period of a socio-technical world, new energies and vitalities must be found. Realizing the American Dream demand an active lifestyle, a creative endeavor, and a new sense of purpose now more than ever, if this Dream is to be kept alive. The world is moving rapidly forward and there is no place for an anemic democracy.

The pace of change demand urgency, an ability to respond appropriately, not only to wars, but to economic, social, and psychological challenges that beset citizens on a daily basis.

It is time for the end of segregation and exclusivity, racism, poverty, and all the other ills so pronounced in America which only dilute the real meaning of the American Dream. These are not impossible achievements and neither do they rely solely on the actions of leaders. Attitudes and behavior will have to change. Thinking and doing must be better aligned, and actions and words must coalesce. If these means can be achieved, maybe a realistic and more pragmatic understanding of the Dream will be forthcoming, and the Great United States of America shall be restored.

Author's Scholarly Booklist

Below is a list of scholarly books done by the Author that is available on Amazon.com in both Soft Cover and for Kindle Edition.

- Henry, B. C. (2010). *Free and open source software, an enabler for strategic alignment through tactical and operational factors.* Scotts Valley, CA: CreateSpace. ISBN-1456308386

- Henry, B. C. (2010). *Leadership, a practical guide to theory and practice.* Scotts Valley, CA: CreateSpace. ISBN-145632036X

- Henry, B. C. (2010). *Philosophy explained: Constructing meaning.* Scotts Valley, CA: CreateSpace. ISBN-1456331310

NOTES